Mastering

BOLLINGER BANDS

A Comprehensive Guide to Trading Strategies

From Basic to Advanced

by

Lalit Mohanty

PREFACE

Welcome to "Mastering Bollinger Bands: From Basics to Advanced Strategies." In the fast-paced world of financial markets, mastering technical analysis is a key skill for traders seeking to navigate the complexities of price movements. Bollinger Bands, developed by John Bollinger, have stood the test of time as a versatile and widely-used tool for technical analysis.

This book is a comprehensive guide designed to take you on a journey from the fundamental concepts of Bollinger Bands to advanced strategies and their applications in various market conditions. Whether you are a novice trader looking to grasp the basics or an experienced professional aiming to refine your skills, this book is crafted to meet your needs.

We begin by unraveling the core principles behind Bollinger Bands, exploring their construction, interpretation, and significance in identifying market trends. As we progress, you'll delve into advanced strategies, such as recognizing squeeze patterns, trading breakouts, and identifying potential reversals.

The exploration doesn't stop there. We'll uncover the synergy of Bollinger Bands with other indicators, delve into algorithmic trading possibilities, and peek into the psychological aspects of trading. Real-life case studies and insights into common mistakes to avoid provide practical wisdom that goes beyond theoretical concepts.

As we navigate the diverse landscape of trading, this book goes beyond the indicator itself. It delves into the regulatory considerations, the integration of Bollinger Bands with emerging technologies, and resources for continuous learning. We've curated a list of recommended books, online courses, and platforms to empower you with the tools needed for effective Bollinger Bands analysis.

Remember, trading is not just about following rules but understanding the dynamics of the markets and adapting to change. This book is more than a guide; it's an invitation to explore, learn, and continuously improve your skills in the fascinating world of technical analysis and trading.

So, whether you're just starting your journey or looking to refine your expertise, let's embark on this exploration of Bollinger Bands together. May your trading endeavors be informed, strategic, and ultimately successful.

Lalit Mohanty

Table of Contents

Chapter 8: Combining Bollinger Bands with Other Indicators

- Moving Averages

- Relative Strength Index (RSI)

- MACD (Moving Average Convergence Divergence)

Chapter 9: Bollinger Bands and Trend Analysis

- Trend Identification with Bollinger Bands

- Trading Trends Effectively

Chapter 10: Advanced Bollinger Bands Strategies

- Multiple Timeframe Analysis

- Fibonacci Retracements with Bollinger Bands

- Mean Reversion Strategies

Chapter 11: Bollinger Bands and Candlestick Patterns

- Japanese Candlestick Patterns

- Bollinger Bands Confirmation with Candlesticks

Chapter 12: Day Trading with Bollinger Bands

- Intraday Strategies

- Scalping Techniques

Chapter 13: Swing Trading Strategies

- Using Bollinger Bands for Swing Trading

- Position Sizing and Risk Management

Chapter 14: Bollinger Bands and Options Trading

- Option Strategies with Bollinger Bands

- Hedging Techniques

Chapter 15: Algorithmic Trading with Bollinger Bands

- Unique Considerations in Cryptocurrency Markets

- Cryptocurrency-Specific Strategies

Chapter 24: Advanced Charting Techniques

- Renko Charts

- Heikin-Ashi Charts

- Point and Figure Charts

Chapter 25: Bollinger Bands and Economic Indicators

- Impact of Economic Data on Bollinger Bands

- Trading Around Economic Events

Chapter 26: Regulatory Considerations

- Compliance and Regulations in Trading

- Staying Informed about Market Changes

Chapter 27: Future Developments in Bollinger Bands

- Emerging Trends and Technologies

- Evolution of Trading Strategies

Chapter 28: Resources and Tools for Bollinger Bands Analysis

- Recommended Books

- Online Courses and Webinars

- Trading Platforms and Software

Chapter 29: Conclusion and Final Thoughts

- Summing Up Key Concepts

- Encouragement for Continuous Learning and Improvement

CHAPTER 1

INTRODUCTION TO BOLLINGER BANDS

Definition and Origin

Bollinger Bands, developed by renowned technical analyst John Bollinger in the 1980s, are a versatile and widely used technical indicator in financial markets. These bands are primarily employed to analyze and understand the volatility and price movements of a financial instrument. The concept behind Bollinger Bands is rooted in the notion that market prices tend to stay within a certain range and exhibit cyclical patterns. By identifying these patterns, traders can make more informed decisions regarding potential price movements.

At its core, Bollinger Bands consist of three key components: a simple moving average (SMA), an upper band, and a lower band. The upper and lower bands are plotted based on the standard deviation of price movements from the SMA. This volatility-based approach allows traders to visualize the expansion or contraction of price ranges over a specified period, aiding in the identification of potential trend reversals, breakouts, and periods of consolidation.

Components of Bollinger Bands

1. **Simple Moving Average (SMA):** The foundation of Bollinger Bands is the SMA, representing the average closing price of an asset over a defined period. Commonly, a 20-period SMA is utilized, but traders may adjust this parameter based on their specific preferences and trading objectives.

2. **Upper Band:** The upper band is constructed by adding a multiple of the standard deviation to the SMA. The standard deviation is a statistical measure of the dispersion of prices from the average. Typically, a multiplier of 2 is applied, resulting in the upper band representing a level that is two standard deviations above the SMA.

3. **Lower Band:** Similarly, the lower band is created by subtracting a multiple of the standard deviation from the SMA. Using the same multiplier of 2, the lower

band signifies a level that is two standard deviations below the SMA.

Purpose and Significance in Trading

The primary purpose of Bollinger Bands is to provide traders with a visual representation of price volatility and potential turning points in the market. By dynamically adjusting to market conditions, Bollinger Bands adapt to varying levels of volatility, making them an invaluable tool for traders across different timeframes.

Key Significances:

1. **Volatility Identification:** Bollinger Bands excel at highlighting periods of increased or decreased market volatility. Expanded bands suggest higher volatility, while contracted bands indicate lower volatility.

2. **Overbought and Oversold Conditions:** Bollinger Bands are frequently utilized to identify overbought and oversold conditions in the market. Prices touching or surpassing the upper band may suggest overbought conditions, while prices touching or falling below the lower band may indicate oversold conditions.

3. **Trend Analysis:** The relationship between price and the bands aids in identifying trends. Prices consistently riding the upper band may signify an uptrend, while those hugging the lower band may suggest a downtrend.

4. **Reversal Signals:** Bollinger Bands can provide early signals of potential trend reversals, especially during periods of extreme volatility or when prices touch the bands.

In conclusion, Bollinger Bands offer traders a comprehensive framework for assessing market conditions, identifying potential entry and exit points, and managing risk effectively. As we delve deeper into subsequent chapters, we will explore various strategies and applications that leverage the power of Bollinger Bands in trading.

CHAPTER 2

UNDERSTANDING MARKET VOLATILITY

Relationship between Bollinger Bands and Market Volatility

Volatility is a critical concept in financial markets, influencing the degree of uncertainty and risk associated with price movements. Understanding the relationship between Bollinger Bands and market volatility is essential for traders seeking to navigate dynamic market conditions successfully.

Bollinger Bands are inherently tied to market volatility. The bands dynamically adjust to the level of price volatility, expanding during periods of increased volatility and contracting when the market is relatively calm. The central premise is that volatility tends to be cyclical, with periods of high volatility often followed by relative calmness and vice versa.

In times of heightened volatility, the distance between the upper and lower bands widens. This signifies larger price swings and greater market uncertainty. Traders can interpret this expansion as an opportunity for potential trend movements, breakouts, or reversals. Conversely, during periods of low volatility, the bands contract, indicating a more stable market environment where prices are less likely to experience significant fluctuations.

By observing the behavior of Bollinger Bands, traders gain valuable insights into the prevailing market conditions. Recognizing volatility patterns allows for the implementation of appropriate trading strategies, such as adapting position sizes, adjusting risk management parameters, and selecting trading approaches that align with the current market environment.

Volatility Indicators

While Bollinger Bands themselves are a form of volatility indicator, traders often complement their analysis with additional tools specifically designed to measure and quantify market volatility. These indicators provide a more nuanced understanding of volatility dynamics and aid in fine-tuning trading decisions.

1. **Average True Range (ATR)**: ATR is a popular volatility indicator that measures the average range

between high and low prices over a specified period. Traders use ATR to gauge the level of volatility, helping them set stop-loss levels and determine the potential magnitude of price movements.

2. **Volatility Index (VIX):** Known as the "fear index," VIX measures the market's expectation of future volatility. A rising VIX suggests increased uncertainty and potential market turbulence, while a declining VIX indicates greater market confidence and lower expected volatility.

3. **Standard Deviation:** Bollinger Bands themselves incorporate standard deviation as a measure of price dispersion. Traders can use standard deviation as a standalone indicator to assess the magnitude of price movements and volatility.

4. **Chandelier Exit:** This indicator, based on ATR, helps traders identify potential exit points by considering volatility. It adjusts the exit point based on market volatility, providing a dynamic trailing stop.

5. **Bollinger Band Width:** Derived directly from Bollinger Bands, the Band Width indicator quantifies the percentage difference between the upper and lower bands. A narrowing Band Width signals decreasing volatility, while an expanding Band Width suggests increasing volatility.

Understanding and effectively utilizing these volatility indicators in conjunction with Bollinger Bands empower traders to make informed decisions in response to changing market conditions. As we progress through this guide, we will explore practical applications and strategies that leverage volatility insights for successful trading.

CHAPTER 3

CONSTRUCTION OF BOLLINGER BANDS

Bollinger Bands serve as a powerful tool for traders, and understanding their construction is fundamental to unlocking their potential. This chapter delves into the intricate details of how Bollinger Bands are formulated and the key parameters involved.

Formula and Calculation

The construction of Bollinger Bands involves three primary components: a simple moving average (SMA), an upper band, and a lower band. These bands are derived from the standard deviation of price movements around the SMA.

1. **Simple Moving Average (SMA):** The foundation of Bollinger Bands is the SMA, calculated by summing up

a set number of closing prices and dividing the sum by the chosen period. For instance, a 20-period SMA considers the closing prices of the last 20 periods and computes their average.

Formula:

$$SMA = \sum_{i=1}^{n} \frac{Closing\ Price\ i}{n}$$

Closing Price

2. **Upper Band:** The upper band is calculated by adding a multiple of the standard deviation to the SMA. Typically, a multiplier of 2 is used, representing two standard deviations above the SMA.

Formula:
Upper Band=SMA+(2×Standard Deviation)Upper Band=SMA+(2×Standard Deviation)

3. **Lower Band:** Similarly, the lower band is derived by subtracting a multiple of the standard deviation from the SMA. Using the same multiplier of 2, the lower band represents two standard deviations below the SMA.

Formula:
Lower Band=SMA−(2×Standard Deviation)Lower Band=SMA−(2×Standard Deviation)

The standard deviation measures the dispersion of closing prices from the SMA, providing insight into the volatility of the asset. A higher standard deviation results in wider bands, indicating increased volatility, while a lower standard deviation leads to narrower bands, signifying lower volatility.

Parameters: Period, Standard Deviation, and Moving Averages

1. **Period:** The period is a crucial parameter that determines the number of data points considered in the calculation of the SMA and standard deviation. Commonly, a 20-period setting is employed, but traders may adjust this value based on their trading style, preferences, and the timeframe they are analyzing. Shorter periods lead to more responsive bands, while longer periods offer a smoother representation of price movements.

2. **Standard Deviation:** The standard deviation is a measure of the dispersion of closing prices around the SMA. The use of a 2-standard deviation multiplier is customary in Bollinger Bands construction, as it captures approximately 95% of the data within the bands, aligning with the statistical concept of normal distribution.

3. **Moving Averages:** Bollinger Bands incorporate a simple moving average as a baseline to represent the average price over a specified period. The choice of

the moving average type (simple, exponential, etc.) is left to the trader's discretion. The 20-period simple moving average is widely accepted, but experimentation and adaptation to different market conditions are encouraged.

Understanding the interplay of these parameters is pivotal for traders looking to effectively apply Bollinger Bands in their analysis. As we progress through this guide, we will explore practical strategies and techniques that leverage these components for insightful and actionable trading decisions.

CHAPTER 4

BASIC INTERPRETATION OF BOLLINGER BANDS

Bollinger Bands provide a wealth of information to traders, and mastering their basic interpretation is key to unlocking their potential. This chapter explores the core components of Bollinger Bands and their application in identifying overbought and oversold conditions, as well as trend identification.

Upper Band, Lower Band, and Middle Band

1. **Upper Band:** The upper band of the Bollinger Bands represents the upper limit of the expected price range. It is calculated by adding a multiple (typically 2) of the standard deviation to the simple moving

average (SMA). This band serves as a resistance level, indicating that prices are statistically high and may be due for a reversal or consolidation.

2. **Lower Band:** Conversely, the lower band signifies the lower limit of the expected price range. It is calculated by subtracting a multiple (again, typically 2) of the standard deviation from the SMA. The lower band acts as a support level, suggesting that prices are statistically low and may be poised for a reversal or bounce.

3. **Middle Band:** The middle band is the simple moving average itself. It provides a baseline and represents the average price over the chosen period. As prices oscillate around the middle band, traders can discern the prevailing trend and potential turning points.

Overbought and Oversold Conditions

Bollinger Bands are widely employed to identify overbought and oversold conditions in the market. These conditions are determined based on the relationship between the current price and the position of the bands.

1. **Overbought Conditions:** When prices touch or exceed the upper band, it is considered an overbought condition. This suggests that the asset may be overvalued, and a reversal or pullback could be imminent. Traders often interpret overbought

conditions as a signal to consider selling or taking profits.

2. **Oversold Conditions:** Conversely, when prices touch or fall below the lower band, it is deemed an oversold condition. This indicates that the asset may be undervalued, and a potential reversal or bounce may be in the offing. Traders viewing oversold conditions may consider buying or taking long positions.

Trend Identification

Bollinger Bands are valuable for discerning the prevailing trend and potential trend reversals. The relationship between price and the bands aids in identifying different market scenarios:

1. **Uptrend:** In an uptrend, prices tend to ride the upper band. As the trend strengthens, the upper band acts as dynamic support, and prices remain above the middle band.

2. **Downtrend:** Conversely, in a downtrend, prices often hug the lower band. The lower band serves as dynamic resistance, and prices stay below the middle band as the downtrend continues.

3. **Sideways or Range-Bound Market:** During periods of consolidation or a sideways market, prices fluctuate between the upper and lower bands, and the middle band may act as both support and resistance.

CHAPTER 5

BOLLINGER BANDS SQUEEZE

Bollinger Bands Squeeze is a distinctive market condition that provides valuable insights into potential explosive price movements. This chapter explores the characteristics of a Bollinger Bands Squeeze, how to recognize squeeze patterns, and the trading opportunities that arise during these periods.

Recognizing Squeeze Patterns

The Bollinger Bands Squeeze occurs when the bands contract tightly, signifying a period of low volatility and a potential buildup of energy for a significant price movement. The contraction of the bands is visualized on the price chart as the upper and lower bands come closer together, creating a narrowing range. This contraction is indicative of a market in a state of temporary equilibrium, with supply and demand forces reaching a balance.

Key characteristics of a Bollinger Bands Squeeze include:

1. **Narrowing Band Width:** The Band Width, which measures the percentage difference between the upper and lower bands, contracts to historically low levels. This narrowing suggests that the price range has compressed, and a breakout or significant price movement may be imminent.

2. **Decreased Volatility:** During a squeeze, the standard deviation decreases, reflecting reduced price volatility. Traders often compare the current Band Width to historical values to identify unusual contractions that may precede substantial price movements.

3. **Squeeze Duration:** The duration of a squeeze can vary. Shorter squeezes may indicate brief periods of consolidation, while more prolonged squeezes may precede more extended and potentially more significant price trends.

Trading Opportunities during Squeeze

Trading during a Bollinger Bands Squeeze involves anticipating an impending breakout or a sharp price movement. Here are strategies to consider:

1. **Wait for the Breakout:** Traders often wait for the price to break above the upper band or below the lower band before initiating a trade. This breakout can signal the start of a new trend or the continuation of an existing one.

2. **Use Additional Confirmations:** While a squeeze itself is a compelling signal, traders often wait for additional confirmations before entering a trade. This may include observing other technical indicators, monitoring volume patterns, or waiting for a close above or below the bands.

3. **Implement Trend Following Strategies:** If the breakout confirms the beginning of a new trend, traders may employ trend-following strategies. For an upside breakout, this could involve buying, while a downside breakout may trigger short-selling.

4. **Set Tight Stop Losses:** Given the potential for rapid and significant price movements following a squeeze, traders should implement tight stop-loss orders to manage risk effectively.

5. **Consider Option Strategies:** Traders versed in options may explore strategies like straddle or

strangle positions, which involve simultaneously buying or selling both a call and a put option to profit from significant price movements.

It's important to note that not all squeezes lead to major breakouts, and false signals can occur. Traders should use additional analysis and risk management strategies to enhance the effectiveness of their Bollinger Bands Squeeze trades.

CHAPTER 6

BOLLINGER BANDS BREAKOUTS

Bollinger Bands Breakouts represent a significant trading opportunity, signaling the potential start of a new trend or a continuation of an existing one. In this chapter, we explore the methods for identifying breakouts and strategies for trading them effectively.

Identifying Breakouts

Breakouts occur when the price of an asset moves beyond the upper or lower Bollinger Band, signaling a shift in market sentiment and the potential initiation of a new trend. Identifying breakouts requires careful observation of price action and confirmation from other technical indicators. Here are key steps to identify breakouts:

1. **Price Confirmation:** A decisive close above the upper band can signal a potential bullish breakout, while a close below the lower band may indicate a bearish breakout. The strength and significance of the breakout are often correlated with the size of the price move and the volume accompanying it.

2. **Volume Analysis:** Breakouts accompanied by high trading volume tend to be more reliable. Volume serves as a confirmation of market participation and conviction in the new price direction.

3. **Divergence Confirmation:** Confirming a breakout with other technical indicators such as the Relative Strength Index (RSI) or Moving Average Convergence Divergence (MACD) can enhance confidence in the validity of the breakout.

4. **Sustained Move:** A successful breakout is characterized by a sustained move beyond the bands. Traders look for confirmation that the price is not merely touching the band momentarily but is establishing a trend in the breakout direction.

Strategies for Trading Breakouts

1. **Trend Following Strategies:**

- **Buy on Upper Band Breakout (Bullish):** Enter a long position when the price closes convincingly above the upper band, signaling a potential uptrend.

- **Sell on Lower Band Breakout (Bearish):** Initiate a short position when the price closes decisively below the lower band, indicating a potential downtrend.

2. **Reversal Strategies:**

- **Fade the Breakout:** Some traders may adopt a contrarian approach, fading the breakout and expecting a reversal. This strategy requires close monitoring and disciplined risk management.

3. **Volatility Breakout Strategies:**

- **Wait for Increased Volatility:** Enter a trade only when volatility increases, as measured by an expansion in the Band Width. This can help filter out false breakouts during low volatility periods.

4. **Bollinger Band Squeeze Breakouts:**

- **Combine with Squeeze Patterns:** Utilize the Bollinger Bands Squeeze pattern as a precursor to breakouts. Trade the subsequent breakout in the direction of the squeeze.

5. **Use Multiple Timeframes:**

   - **Confirm Breakouts Across Timeframes:** Confirm breakouts by analyzing price action on multiple timeframes. A breakout on a higher timeframe provides more significant confirmation.

6. **Combine with Other Indicators:**

   - **Confirmation with Oscillators:** Use oscillators like the RSI or Stochastic Oscillator to confirm the strength of the breakout. A divergence or confirmation from these indicators can enhance the robustness of the trade.

7. **Risk Management:**

   - **Set Stop Losses:** Implement tight stop-loss orders to manage risk. The volatility associated with breakouts can result in swift reversals, making risk management crucial.

8. **Evaluate the Overall Market Context:**

   - **Consider Market Conditions:** Assess broader market conditions and economic factors to ensure that the breakout aligns with the prevailing market sentiment.

Successfully trading Bollinger Bands breakouts requires a combination of technical analysis, risk management, and a disciplined approach. Traders should adapt strategies to their trading style and timeframe preferences while remaining vigilant for false signals. As we progress in this guide, we will explore advanced techniques for incorporating Bollinger Bands into a comprehensive trading strategy.

CHAPTER 7

BOLLINGER BANDS REVERSALS

Bollinger Bands Reversals mark potential turning points in the market, presenting traders with opportunities to capitalize on a shift in trend direction. This chapter explores the recognition of reversal patterns using Bollinger Bands and introduces confirmation indicators to enhance the accuracy of reversal signals.

Recognizing Reversal Patterns

Reversals using Bollinger Bands involve identifying signs that the current trend may be losing momentum and that a new trend in the opposite direction could be emerging. Key reversal patterns include:

1. **Double Top and Double Bottom:**

- **Double Top (Bearish Reversal):** This pattern occurs when the price reaches a peak, retreats, rallies again to a similar high, and then experiences a significant decline. The lower band can act as a support level.

- **Double Bottom (Bullish Reversal):** In contrast, a double bottom forms when the price reaches a low, bounces, falls to a similar low, and then experiences a notable rally. The upper band may serve as a resistance level.

2. **Head and Shoulders:**

- **Head and Shoulders (Bearish Reversal):** This classic pattern consists of three peaks – a higher peak (head) between two lower peaks (shoulders). A breakdown below the neckline, often near the lower Bollinger Band, signals a potential reversal.

3. **Inverse Head and Shoulders:**

- **Inverse Head and Shoulders (Bullish Reversal):** Mirroring the regular head and shoulders pattern, the inverse head and shoulders have three troughs, with the middle one (head) being lower than the others. A breakout above the neckline, usually near the upper Bollinger Band, indicates a potential bullish reversal.

4. **Divergence with Oscillators:**

- **Bearish Divergence:** If prices are making new highs while an oscillator like the RSI is making lower highs, it may signal weakening bullish momentum and a potential bearish reversal.

- **Bullish Divergence:** Conversely, if prices are making new lows while the oscillator is forming higher lows, it may indicate weakening bearish momentum and a potential bullish reversal.

Confirmation Indicators

While recognizing reversal patterns is a crucial first step, traders often seek confirmation from additional indicators to increase the reliability of the reversal signal. Common confirmation indicators include:

1. **Volume Analysis:**

- **Increase in Volume:** A surge in trading volume accompanying a reversal pattern strengthens the signal. It suggests increased market participation and conviction in the potential trend reversal.

2. **Candlestick Patterns:**

- **Engulfing Patterns:** Bullish engulfing patterns at the lower Bollinger Band and bearish engulfing patterns at the upper Bollinger Band can confirm reversal signals.

3. **Moving Averages:**

   - **Death Cross and Golden Cross:** The Death Cross (short-term moving average crossing below the long-term moving average) may confirm a bearish reversal, while the Golden Cross (short-term moving average crossing above the long-term moving average) may confirm a bullish reversal.

4. **Trendline Breaks:**

   - **Break of Trendlines:** Drawing trendlines connecting peaks or troughs can provide additional confirmation. A breakout above a downtrend line or below an uptrend line aligns with a potential reversal.

5. **Fibonacci Retracements:**

   - **Retracement Levels:** Fibonacci retracement levels can be used to identify potential reversal zones. A reversal signal near a key Fibonacci level strengthens the overall reversal case.

6. **Support and Resistance Levels:**

   - **Confirmation from Key Levels:** A reversal pattern occurring near significant support or resistance levels adds weight to the reversal signal.

By combining recognition of reversal patterns with confirmation indicators, traders can enhance the accuracy of their reversal signals. It's essential to exercise patience and wait for multiple confirmations before entering a trade based on potential reversals. As we progress in this guide, we will explore advanced strategies for integrating Bollinger Bands into comprehensive trading systems.

CHAPTER 8

COMBINING BOLLINGER BANDS WITH OTHER INDICATORS

Integrating Bollinger Bands with other technical indicators can provide traders with a more comprehensive view of market conditions and enhance the accuracy of trading signals. This chapter explores the synergies between Bollinger Bands and three key indicators: Moving Averages, Relative Strength Index (RSI), and MACD (Moving Average Convergence Divergence).

Moving Averages

Bollinger Bands and Moving Averages are often used together to smooth price data and provide a clearer picture of the prevailing trend.

1. **Golden Cross and Death Cross:**

- **Golden Cross (Bullish Signal):** Occurs when the short-term moving average crosses above the long-term moving average. Traders may look for this cross above the lower Bollinger Band as a potential bullish signal.

- **Death Cross (Bearish Signal):** Occurs when the short-term moving average crosses below the long-term moving average. A death cross below the upper Bollinger Band may signal a potential bearish reversal.

2. **Moving Average Envelopes:**

- **Combining Bollinger Bands with Envelopes:** Some traders use Moving Average Envelopes, which are bands plotted above and below a moving average, in conjunction with Bollinger Bands. This combination provides additional insights into potential overbought or oversold conditions.

Relative Strength Index (RSI)

RSI is a momentum oscillator that measures the speed and change of price movements. Combining RSI with Bollinger Bands adds depth to trend analysis and helps identify potential reversal points.

1. **Overbought and Oversold Conditions:**

- **Confirmation with Bollinger Bands:** When RSI indicates overbought conditions (above 70) and the price is touching or exceeding the upper Bollinger Band, it may signal a potential reversal. Conversely, RSI in oversold conditions (below 30) combined with the price touching or falling below the lower Bollinger Band can suggest a potential bullish reversal.

2. **Divergence:**

- **Bollinger Bands Confirmation:** Divergence between RSI and price movements, coupled with confirmation from Bollinger Bands, can enhance the likelihood of a trend reversal. For example, if prices are making new highs, but RSI is not confirming, and the price is touching the upper Bollinger Band, it may signal a bearish reversal.

MACD (Moving Average Convergence Divergence)

MACD is a trend-following momentum indicator that shows the relationship between two moving averages of an asset's price. Combining MACD with Bollinger Bands helps identify trend strength and potential reversals.

1. **MACD Histogram and Signal Line:**

- **Crosses with Bollinger Bands:** Bullish crossovers of the MACD histogram above the signal line, especially when prices are near the lower Bollinger Band, can signal potential buying opportunities. Bearish crossovers below the signal line, especially near the upper Bollinger Band, may indicate potential selling opportunities.

2. **MACD Divergence:**

- **Confirmation with Bollinger Bands:** Divergence between MACD and price movements, corroborated by Bollinger Bands, can strengthen reversal signals. For instance, if prices are making new highs, but MACD is not confirming, and the price is touching the upper Bollinger Band, it may suggest a potential bearish reversal.

Conclusion: Combining Bollinger Bands with Moving Averages, RSI, and MACD provides a multi-faceted approach to technical analysis. Traders benefit from a more nuanced understanding of market conditions and can make well-informed decisions by incorporating signals from multiple indicators. As we progress in this guide, we will explore advanced strategies that leverage the synergies between Bollinger Bands and various technical tools.

CHAPTER 9

BOLLINGER BANDS AND TREND ANALYSIS

Bollinger Bands are powerful tools for trend analysis, aiding traders in identifying trends and making informed decisions based on market dynamics. This chapter explores the use of Bollinger Bands for trend identification and provides strategies for trading trends effectively.

Trend Identification with Bollinger Bands

1. **Riding the Bands:**

   - **Uptrend Identification:** In an uptrend, prices tend to ride the upper band. As the trend strengthens, the upper band acts as dynamic support, and prices remain above the middle band.

- **Downtrend Identification:** Conversely, in a downtrend, prices often hug the lower band. The lower band serves as dynamic resistance, and prices stay below the middle band as the downtrend continues.

- **Sideways Market Identification:** During periods of consolidation or a sideways market, prices fluctuate between the upper and lower bands, and the middle band may act as both support and resistance.

2. **Bollinger Band Squeeze and Trend Reversals:**

- **Squeeze Patterns:** A Bollinger Band Squeeze often precedes a trend reversal. As the bands contract, indicating reduced volatility, traders should be prepared for a potential breakout that could mark the beginning of a new trend.

3. **Trendline Confirmation:**

- **Drawing Trendlines:** Drawing trendlines connecting peaks or troughs can provide additional confirmation of the prevailing trend. A breakout above a downtrend line or below an uptrend line aligns with a potential reversal.

Trading Trends Effectively

1. **Trend Following Strategies:**

- **Moving Averages and Bollinger Bands:** Combine Bollinger Bands with moving averages for trend following. Buy when the price is above both the upper band and a rising moving average, and sell when the price is below both the lower band and a declining moving average.

2. **Bollinger Band Width for Volatility:**

- **Volatility and Trend Strength:** Use the Band Width indicator to gauge volatility. Expanding bands indicate increased volatility, often accompanying strong trends. Traders may enter or add to positions when volatility is high.

3. **Trend Confirmation with RSI:**

- **RSI Confirmation:** Confirm trend strength using the Relative Strength Index (RSI). In an uptrend, RSI values above 50 confirm bullish momentum, while in a downtrend, RSI values below 50 confirm bearish momentum.

4. **Multiple Timeframe Analysis:**

- **Confirmation Across Timeframes:** Analyzing trends on multiple timeframes enhances confidence in trend direction. A trend on a higher timeframe provides more significant confirmation than a trend on a lower timeframe.

5. **Bollinger Bands and Candlestick Patterns:**

   - **Candlestick Confirmation:** Confirm trend reversals or continuations with candlestick patterns. For example, a bullish engulfing pattern near the lower Bollinger Band may confirm a potential reversal in an uptrend.

6. **Use Trailing Stops:**

   - **Trailing Stop Management:** As trends progress, use trailing stops to secure profits while allowing the trend to develop. Trailing stops can be set based on a percentage of price movements or key technical levels.

7. **Avoid Counter-Trend Trading:**

   - **Risk in Counter-Trend Trading:** While counter-trend trading can be profitable, it involves higher risk. Traders should exercise caution and use additional confirmation indicators when considering counter-trend positions.

8. **Distinguish Between Healthy Pullbacks and Reversals:**

   - **Analyzing Pullbacks:** Understand the difference between healthy pullbacks in a trend and potential trend reversals. Bollinger Bands help identify the extent of pullbacks and whether they align with the overall trend.

In conclusion, Bollinger Bands provide traders with a versatile tool for trend analysis. By combining Bollinger Bands with other indicators and adopting effective trend-following strategies, traders can navigate markets with greater confidence and make more informed decisions during various stages of a trend. As we delve into more advanced topics, we will explore additional techniques for optimizing trend analysis with Bollinger Bands.

CHAPTER 10

ADVANCED BOLLINGER BANDS STRATEGIES

Bollinger Bands, when used in advanced strategies, offer traders a deeper understanding of market dynamics and more sophisticated tools for decision-making. This chapter explores advanced strategies involving Multiple Timeframe Analysis, Fibonacci Retracements, and Mean Reversion.

Multiple Timeframe Analysis

1. **Higher Timeframe Confirmation:**

    - **Long-Term Trends:** Analyzing longer timeframes, such as daily or weekly charts, provides a broader perspective on the prevailing trend. Traders can use the higher timeframe trend as a guide for their trading decisions on shorter timeframes.

2. **Confirmation Across Multiple Timeframes:**

   - **Aligning Trends:** A trend identified on a shorter timeframe gains strength and validity when it aligns with the trend on a higher timeframe. For example, if the daily chart indicates an uptrend and the hourly chart confirms it, it adds conviction to bullish trades.

3. **Entry and Exit Timing:**

   - **Precision Timing:** Use a higher timeframe for trend direction and a lower timeframe for precise entry and exit points. This approach allows traders to benefit from the overall trend while fine-tuning entries based on shorter-term price movements.

Fibonacci Retracements with Bollinger Bands

1. **Identifying Potential Reversal Zones:**

   - **Key Fibonacci Levels:** Use Fibonacci retracement levels in conjunction with Bollinger Bands to identify potential reversal zones. For example, a pullback to the 50% retracement level near the lower Bollinger Band may signal a bounce in an uptrend.

2. **Confluence of Support or Resistance:**

- **Bollinger Bands as Dynamic Levels:** Consider the midline of the Bollinger Bands as a dynamic level that aligns with Fibonacci retracement levels. When a Fibonacci level coincides with the midline, it enhances the significance of that level as potential support or resistance.

3. **Bollinger Band Width and Fibonacci Expansion:**

- **Expansion Signals:** Use the Band Width indicator to identify periods of low volatility. When the Band Width is at historical lows, it may precede a significant price movement. Combining this with Fibonacci expansion levels can help identify potential breakout or breakdown points.

Mean Reversion Strategies

1. **Identifying Overextended Moves:**

- **Bollinger Bands Width as an Overextension Indicator:** When Bollinger Bands contract significantly, it suggests low volatility and a potential period of consolidation. Traders can anticipate a mean reversion to the middle band as volatility expands.

2. **Combining Mean Reversion with RSI:**

- **Oversold or Overbought Conditions:** Combine Bollinger Bands with the Relative Strength

Index (RSI) to identify oversold or overbought conditions. A price touching the lower Bollinger Band with RSI below 30 may indicate an oversold condition, while a touch of the upper band with RSI above 70 may indicate overbought conditions.

3. **Reversion to the Mean as a Probability Edge:**

   - **Dynamic Support and Resistance:** View the middle band as a dynamic support or resistance level. When prices deviate significantly from the middle band, there is a higher probability of a reversion to the mean.

4. **Combining with Moving Averages:**

   - **Dual Confirmation:** Combine mean reversion strategies with moving averages for dual confirmation. For instance, entering a trade when prices touch the lower Bollinger Band and the 50-period moving average provides additional confirmation.

5. **Volatility Bands for Mean Reversion:**

   - **Using Volatility Bands:** In addition to traditional Bollinger Bands, consider using volatility bands based on a measure like Average True Range (ATR) for mean reversion. When prices extend beyond the volatility bands, a reversion to the mean becomes more likely.

CHAPTER 11

BOLLINGER BANDS AND CANDLESTICK PATTERNS

Combining Bollinger Bands with Japanese Candlestick Patterns provides traders with a robust approach to analyzing price movements and making informed decisions. This chapter explores the significance of Japanese Candlestick Patterns and how they can be used in conjunction with Bollinger Bands for enhanced confirmation.

Japanese Candlestick Patterns

1. **Bullish Candlestick Patterns:**

   - **Bullish Engulfing Pattern:** A two-candle pattern where the second candle completely engulfs the body of the first candle. It signals a potential reversal from a downtrend to an uptrend.

- **Hammer:** A single candlestick with a small body and a long lower shadow, indicating potential buying pressure after a decline.

- **Bullish Harami:** A two-candle pattern where the first candle is a large bearish candle, followed by a smaller bullish candle completely contained within the range of the first candle.

2. **Bearish Candlestick Patterns:**

- **Bearish Engulfing Pattern:** Similar to the bullish engulfing but signals a potential reversal from an uptrend to a downtrend.

- **Shooting Star:** A single candlestick with a small body and a long upper shadow, indicating potential selling pressure after an advance.

- **Bearish Harami:** The opposite of the bullish harami, where a small bullish candle is engulfed by a larger bearish candle.

3. **Reversal Patterns:**

- **Doji:** A candlestick with a very small body, indicating indecision in the market. A doji near Bollinger Bands may signal potential reversal points.

- **Morning Star:** A three-candle pattern with a large bearish candle, followed by a small indecisive candle, and then a large bullish candle. It suggests a potential reversal from a downtrend to an uptrend.

Bollinger Bands Confirmation with Candlesticks

1. **Engulfing Patterns and Band Touch:**

   - **Bullish Engulfing Near Lower Band:** When a bullish engulfing pattern occurs near the lower Bollinger Band, it adds confirmation to a potential reversal and suggests a buying opportunity.

   - **Bearish Engulfing Near Upper Band:** Conversely, a bearish engulfing pattern near the upper Bollinger Band may signal a potential reversal and serve as a selling opportunity.

2. **Candlestick Patterns at Band Extremes:**

   - **Shooting Star at Upper Band:** A shooting star candlestick near the upper Bollinger Band adds weight to the idea that prices might reverse, especially if other technical indicators confirm.

   - **Hammer at Lower Band:** A hammer candlestick at the lower Bollinger Band indicates potential buying interest and may signal a reversal.

3. **Doji and Bollinger Bands Squeeze:**

   - **Doji During Squeeze:** A doji candlestick during a Bollinger Bands squeeze may suggest indecision in the market, and traders should be prepared for a potential breakout.

4. **Confirmation with Morning Star and Evening Star:**

   - **Morning Star Formation:** When a morning star pattern occurs near the lower Bollinger Band, it strengthens the case for a potential bullish reversal.

   - **Evening Star Formation:** Conversely, an evening star pattern near the upper Bollinger Band may suggest a potential bearish reversal.

5. **Using Bollinger Bands Width for Confirmation:**

   - **Confirming with Band Width:** Confirm candlestick patterns by assessing Bollinger Bands Width. If a candlestick pattern coincides with a low Band Width, it suggests that the market is in a consolidation phase, and a potential breakout is imminent.

CHAPTER 12

DAY TRADING WITH BOLLINGER BANDS

Day trading with Bollinger Bands offers traders the opportunity to capitalize on short-term price movements and intraday volatility. This chapter explores intraday strategies and scalping techniques using Bollinger Bands.

Intraday Strategies

1. **Bollinger Bands Breakout Strategy:**

   - **Timeframe Selection:** Day traders often use shorter timeframes, such as 5 or 15 minutes. Identify periods of low volatility, characterized by a Bollinger Bands squeeze.

- **Breakout Confirmation:** Enter a trade when prices break above the upper band in an uptrend or below the lower band in a downtrend.

- **Volatility Consideration:** Confirm the breakout with an increase in volume and pay attention to the Band Width, ensuring that the breakout occurs during a period of low volatility.

2. **Moving Average Crossover with Bollinger Bands:**

- **Combining Indicators:** Use a short-term moving average (e.g., 9-period) and a longer-term moving average (e.g., 21-period) in conjunction with Bollinger Bands.

- **Crossover Signals:** Enter a trade when the short-term moving average crosses above the longer-term moving average, and prices are above the upper Bollinger Band for a potential uptrend. Conversely, enter a short trade when the short-term moving average crosses below the longer-term moving average, and prices are below the lower Bollinger Band for a potential downtrend.

3. **Bollinger Bands Reversal Strategy:**

- **Divergence Confirmation:** Look for divergence between price and an oscillator like the Relative

Strength Index (RSI). For example, if prices are making new highs, but RSI is not confirming, and the price touches the upper Bollinger Band, it may suggest a potential reversal.

- **Counter-Trend Entry:** Enter a counter-trend trade when prices touch or exceed the upper Bollinger Band in an uptrend or touch or fall below the lower Bollinger Band in a downtrend.

Scalping Techniques

1. **Bollinger Band Squeeze Scalping:**

   - **Identifying Squeeze Periods:** Scalpers look for periods of low volatility marked by a Bollinger Bands squeeze on very short timeframes (e.g., 1 or 3 minutes).

   - **Breakout Confirmation:** Enter a trade in the direction of the breakout as soon as prices breach the upper or lower Bollinger Band.

   - **Quick Exits:** Scalpers aim for small price movements and often exit positions as soon as a minimal profit target is achieved.

2. **Volatility Bands Scalping:**

   - **Using Volatility Bands:** On very short timeframes, incorporate volatility bands based on indicators like Average True Range (ATR) along with Bollinger Bands.

- **Scalping Within Bands:** Enter and exit trades as prices move within the volatility bands, capitalizing on short-term price fluctuations.

3. **Moving Average Ribbon Scalping:**

   - **Multiple Moving Averages:** Apply a ribbon of short-term moving averages (e.g., 5, 10, 15) to capture short-term trends.

   - **Scalping with Moving Average Crosses:** Enter trades based on the crossovers of these moving averages, aligning with Bollinger Bands for additional confirmation.

4. **Mean Reversion Scalping:**

   - **Identifying Overbought or Oversold Conditions:** Scalpers look for overextended price movements beyond the upper or lower Bollinger Band on short timeframes.

   - **Quick Reversion to the Mean:** Enter trades anticipating a quick reversion to the middle band, capturing small intraday price corrections.

CHAPTER 13

SWING TRADING STRATEGIES

Swing trading with Bollinger Bands combines the benefits of trend-following and mean-reversion approaches, allowing traders to capture price swings over a relatively short to intermediate timeframe. This chapter explores effective swing trading strategies using Bollinger Bands, along with essential considerations such as position sizing and risk management.

Using Bollinger Bands for Swing Trading

1. **Identifying Trend Reversals:**

   - **Reversal Signals:** Look for reversal signals when prices touch or exceed the upper or lower Bollinger Band, especially after a prolonged trend.

- **Divergence Confirmation:** Combine Bollinger Bands with oscillators like the Relative Strength Index (RSI) to confirm divergence, enhancing the likelihood of a trend reversal.

2. **Swing Trading in the Trend:**

   - **Riding the Bands:** In an established trend, use Bollinger Bands to identify pullbacks. Enter trades when prices touch the middle band during an uptrend or the middle band acts as resistance during a downtrend.

3. **Bollinger Bands Breakout Swing Strategy:**

   - **Breakout Confirmation:** Wait for a clear breakout above the upper band for bullish swing trades or below the lower band for bearish swing trades.

   - **Volatility Considerations:** Confirm breakouts with an increase in volume and monitor the Band Width to ensure breakouts occur during periods of low volatility.

4. **Moving Average Crossover for Swing Trading:**

   - **Dual Confirmation:** Combine Bollinger Bands with a moving average crossover strategy. For example, enter a bullish swing trade when prices are above the upper Bollinger Band and the short-term moving average crosses above the long-term moving average.

5. **Fibonacci Retracements with Bollinger Bands:**

   - **Identifying Potential Reversal Zones:** Use Fibonacci retracement levels in conjunction with Bollinger Bands to identify potential reversal zones. For example, a pullback to the 50% retracement level near the lower Bollinger Band may signal a bounce in an uptrend.

Position Sizing and Risk Management

1. **Setting Stop-Loss Orders:**

   - **Volatility-Based Stops:** Utilize the information from Bollinger Bands to set dynamic stop-loss orders. For instance, place a stop below the lower band for long trades and above the upper band for short trades.

   - **Percentage Risk Model:** Implement a percentage risk model, risking a small percentage of the trading capital on each trade, to ensure consistent risk management.

2. **Diversification of Trades:**

   - **Asset and Timeframe Diversification:** Diversify swing trades across different assets and timeframes to spread risk and reduce exposure to individual market dynamics.

- **Correlation Considerations:** Be aware of correlations between assets to avoid overexposure to a particular market or sector.

3. **Using Reward-to-Risk Ratios:**

   - **Risk-Reward Assessment:** Evaluate each swing trade based on the potential reward-to-risk ratio. Ensure that potential profits are substantially larger than potential losses.

   - **Profit Target Placement:** Set profit targets based on key support or resistance levels, previous swing highs or lows, or significant technical levels.

4. **Adaptation to Market Conditions:**

   - **Adjusting Position Sizes:** During periods of high volatility, consider reducing position sizes to account for larger price swings. Conversely, during low volatility, adjust position sizes to accommodate potential smaller price movements.

5. **Regular Portfolio Review:**

   - **Periodic Evaluation:** Regularly review and assess the overall portfolio, analyzing the performance of swing trades, adjusting strategies based on market conditions, and making necessary refinements to risk management.

Swing trading with Bollinger Bands offers a versatile and dynamic approach to capturing medium-term price movements. By integrating effective strategies with robust risk management practices, traders can optimize their swing trading endeavors and navigate the markets with greater confidence. As we conclude this guide, remember that ongoing learning and adaptability are crucial for sustained success in swing trading with Bollinger Bands.

CHAPTER 14

BOLLINGER BANDS AND OPTIONS TRADING

Integrating Bollinger Bands into options trading strategies provides traders with valuable insights into potential price movements and volatility. This chapter explores option strategies with Bollinger Bands, along with effective hedging techniques for risk management.

Option Strategies with Bollinger Bands

1. **Bollinger Bands Squeeze for Option Buying:**

    - **Identifying Low Volatility:** Use Bollinger Bands to recognize periods of low volatility, indicated by a squeeze in the bands. Low volatility often precedes significant price movements.

- **Buying Straddles or Strangles:** Consider buying long straddle or strangle options strategies during a Bollinger Bands squeeze. These strategies involve purchasing both a call and a put with the same expiration date, anticipating a breakout and a subsequent price movement.

2. **Directional Trading with Options:**

   - **Bullish Breakout Strategies:** In anticipation of a bullish breakout, consider buying call options or executing bullish call spreads. Confirm the breakout with an increase in volume.

   - **Bearish Breakout Strategies:** For an expected bearish breakout, consider buying put options or implementing bearish put spreads. Validate the breakout with an uptick in volume.

3. **Iron Condor for Range-Bound Markets:**

   - **Identifying Range-Bound Conditions:** When Bollinger Bands indicate a sideways or range-bound market, employ an iron condor strategy. This involves selling both a put spread and a call spread, capitalizing on the expectation of limited price movement within a specified range.

4. **Combining Bollinger Bands with Delta Hedging:**

- **Delta Hedging for Neutral Strategies:** Delta hedging involves adjusting the position's delta to maintain a neutral stance. In a neutral market, combine delta-hedged strategies with Bollinger Bands for enhanced confirmation.

5. **Using Bollinger Bands for Timing Entry and Exits:**

   - **Bollinger Bands as Entry Signals:** Employ Bollinger Bands to time entry points for option trades. For instance, enter an options trade when prices touch the lower Bollinger Band in an uptrend, suggesting potential support.

   - **Exit Signals:** Consider exiting or adjusting options positions when prices touch or exceed the upper Bollinger Band in an uptrend, indicating potential resistance.

Hedging Techniques

1. **Protective Put for Stock Positions:**

   - **Applying Protective Puts:** If holding a long stock position, use protective puts to hedge against potential downside risk. Purchase put options that act as insurance, limiting potential losses in case of a significant decline.

2. **Collar Strategy with Bollinger Bands Confirmation:**

- **Creating a Collar:** A collar involves simultaneously buying a protective put and selling a covered call. Use Bollinger Bands to confirm entry and exit points for the collar strategy, particularly focusing on potential breakouts.

3. **Calendar Spread Hedging:**

- **Hedging with Calendar Spreads:** Hedging with calendar spreads involves buying and selling options with different expiration dates. Use Bollinger Bands to identify potential turning points and adjust the timing of calendar spread entries.

4. **Dynamic Delta Hedging:**

- **Adjusting Delta Exposure:** Regularly assess and adjust the delta exposure of options positions based on Bollinger Bands signals. Increase or decrease delta exposure as the market conditions and volatility levels change.

5. **Volatility Skew Considerations:**

- **Utilizing Volatility Skew:** Be mindful of volatility skew, the uneven distribution of implied volatility across different strike prices. Adjust option positions and hedges based on Bollinger Bands signals and volatility skew considerations.

CHAPTER 15

ALGORITHMIC TRADING WITH BOLLINGER BANDS

Algorithmic trading leverages computational power to execute trading strategies automatically. Integrating Bollinger Bands into algorithms enhances the sophistication of these strategies. This chapter explores the process of building algorithmic trading systems with Bollinger Bands, along with crucial considerations for backtesting and optimization.

Building Bollinger Bands into Algorithms

1. **Define Clear Trading Rules:**

   - **Strategy Logic:** Clearly articulate the logic of the algorithm, specifying how Bollinger Bands will be used in making trading decisions.

Establish rules for entering, exiting, and managing trades based on Bollinger Bands signals.

2. Parameter Optimization:

- **Optimal Settings:** Determine the optimal parameters for Bollinger Bands, including the period and standard deviation. Conduct thorough testing to identify parameter values that maximize the strategy's performance.

3. Market Conditions Adaptation:

- **Dynamic Adaptation:** Program the algorithm to dynamically adapt to changing market conditions. For instance, adjust the Bollinger Bands parameters during high volatility periods and tighten them during low volatility.

4. Risk Management Integration:

- **Incorporate Risk Controls:** Implement risk management protocols within the algorithm. This includes setting stop-loss levels based on Bollinger Bands signals and adjusting position sizes based on volatility.

5. Multiple Timeframe Analysis:

- **Multi-Timeframe Signals:** Incorporate multiple timeframe analysis into the algorithm. For example, use daily Bollinger Bands for trend direction confirmation and intraday Bollinger Bands for precise entry and exit signals.

6. **Avoid Overfitting:**

- **Balance Complexity:** Strike a balance between model complexity and robustness. Overfitting occurs when an algorithm is excessively tailored to historical data but performs poorly on new data. Regularly review and refine the algorithm to prevent overfitting.

Backtesting and Optimization

1. **Historical Data Collection:**

- **Comprehensive Dataset:** Collect a comprehensive dataset for backtesting, including price data, volume, and other relevant indicators. Ensure the dataset covers various market conditions.

2. **Software and Tools:**

- **Use Reliable Platforms:** Utilize robust backtesting platforms or programming languages like Python with libraries such as pandas, NumPy, and backtrader. Reliable tools help ensure accurate simulation and evaluation of the algorithm's performance.

3. **Backtesting Strategy Execution:**

- **Simulate Real Market Conditions:** Implement the algorithm in a simulated environment that replicates real market conditions. This includes factoring in transaction costs, slippage, and order execution delays.

4. **Performance Metrics:**

- **Evaluate Metrics:** Assess the algorithm's performance using various metrics, including returns, drawdowns, Sharpe ratio, and win-loss ratios. These metrics provide insights into the strategy's profitability and risk.

5. **Walk-Forward Testing:**

- **Dynamic Optimization:** Perform walk-forward testing to dynamically optimize the algorithm as it progresses through different time periods. This helps adapt the strategy to evolving market conditions.

6. **Monte Carlo Simulations:**

- **Scenario Analysis:** Conduct Monte Carlo simulations to analyze the algorithm's performance under various market scenarios. This provides a more comprehensive understanding of the strategy's robustness.

7. **Risk Assessment:**

- **Stress Testing:** Subject the algorithm to stress testing by simulating extreme market conditions. Evaluate how the strategy behaves during periods of high volatility or unexpected events.

8. **Continuous Monitoring and Adjustment:**

    - **Adaptation to Changing Markets:** Continuously monitor the algorithm's performance and adjust parameters based on ongoing market dynamics. Regularly review and update the strategy to ensure it remains effective.

CHAPTER 16

REAL-LIFE CASE STUDIES

Examining real-life case studies offers invaluable insights into the practical application of Bollinger Bands in trading. This chapter delves into both successful trades that showcase the effectiveness of Bollinger Bands and instances where failures occurred, emphasizing the importance of learning from mistakes.

Examining Successful Trades

1. **Trade 1: Trend Confirmation with Bollinger Bands**

   - **Context:** A stock is in a well-established uptrend.

   - **Bollinger Bands Use:** Buy signals are generated when the price touches the lower band and the trend is confirmed by the Relative Strength Index (RSI).

- **Outcome:** The stock bounces off the lower Bollinger Band, and RSI confirms strong bullish momentum. The trade results in a profitable uptrend capture.

2. **Trade 2: Bollinger Bands Squeeze Breakout**

   - **Context:** A period of low volatility is identified through a Bollinger Bands squeeze.

   - **Bollinger Bands Use:** Execute trades upon a breakout above the upper band.

   - **Outcome:** The breakout is accompanied by a surge in volume, leading to a significant price movement. The trade results in a profitable capture of the volatility expansion.

3. **Trade 3: Mean Reversion in a Range-Bound Market**

   - **Context:** A stock is trading within a well-defined range.

   - **Bollinger Bands Use:** Sell signals are generated when the price touches the upper band, anticipating a mean reversion to the middle band.

- **Outcome:** The stock reverts to the middle band, resulting in a profitable trade capturing the price oscillations within the range.

Analyzing Failures and Learning from Mistakes

1. **Trade 1: Ignoring Overall Market Conditions**

   - **Mistake:** Failing to consider broader market trends and economic conditions.

   - **Outcome:** Despite a strong setup according to Bollinger Bands, the trade fails as overall market conditions were bearish. Lesson: Always assess the macroeconomic environment before entering trades.

2. **Trade 2: Overlooking Multiple Timeframes**

   - **Mistake:** Ignoring signals on higher timeframes.

   - **Outcome:** The trade fails as the trader only considers short-term Bollinger Bands signals, missing a significant trend reversal on a higher timeframe. Lesson: Incorporate multiple timeframes for comprehensive analysis.

3. **Trade 3: Lack of Confirmation from Other Indicators**

   - **Mistake:** Relying solely on Bollinger Bands without confirmation from other indicators.

- **Outcome:** The trade fails as there is no confirmation from oscillators or other technical indicators. Lesson: Use Bollinger Bands in conjunction with complementary tools for stronger signals.

4. **Trade 4: Poor Risk Management**

   - **Mistake:** Neglecting proper risk management principles.

   - **Outcome:** Despite a strong Bollinger Bands setup, the trade results in a significant loss due to inadequate risk management. Lesson: Set realistic stop-loss levels and position sizes based on risk tolerance.

5. **Trade 5: Chasing the Squeeze without Confirmation**

   - **Mistake:** Entering trades solely based on a Bollinger Bands squeeze without confirming signals.

   - **Outcome:** The anticipated breakout never materializes, leading to a losing trade. Lesson: Confirm squeeze patterns with volume and additional technical indicators before entering trades.

6. **Trade 6: Failing to Adapt to Changing Volatility**

- **Mistake:** Neglecting to adjust Bollinger Bands parameters during periods of changing volatility.

- **Outcome:** The strategy fails to adapt to increased volatility, resulting in losses during a volatile market phase. Lesson: Regularly reassess and adapt Bollinger Bands parameters based on evolving market conditions.

CHAPTER 17

PSYCHOLOGICAL ASPECTS OF TRADING WITH BOLLINGER BANDS

While technical analysis, including tools like Bollinger Bands, provides a structured approach to trading, the psychological aspects play a critical role in a trader's success. This chapter explores the importance of discipline, patience, and emotional control when incorporating Bollinger Bands into trading strategies.

Discipline and Patience

1. **Understanding Market Dynamics:**

   - **Disciplined Observation:** Disciplined traders understand that markets can be unpredictable. Bollinger Bands provide a framework, but success requires patience and a disciplined approach to interpreting signals in the context of broader market dynamics.

2. **Adhering to Trading Plans:**

- **Rule-Based Trading:** Bollinger Bands work best within a well-defined trading plan. Discipline involves adhering to predefined rules for entry, exit, and risk management. Traders should resist the temptation to deviate from their plan based on emotional impulses.

3. **Avoiding Impulsive Decisions:**

- **Patience in Decision-Making:** Patience is the antidote to impulsive decision-making. Waiting for clear Bollinger Bands signals and confirming indicators reduces the likelihood of entering trades hastily. Disciplined traders wait for optimal setups.

4. **Managing Expectations:**

- **Realistic Expectations:** Discipline requires setting realistic expectations. Traders should recognize that not every trade will be a winner, and losses are part of the trading process. A disciplined mindset helps traders weather inevitable ups and downs.

Emotional Control in Trading

1. **Dealing with Losses:**

- **Accepting Losses:** Losses are an inherent part of trading. Emotional control involves accepting losses gracefully, learning from them, and not letting them disrupt the overall trading strategy.

2. **Handling Winning Streaks:**

   - **Avoiding Overconfidence:** Winning streaks can lead to overconfidence, prompting traders to deviate from their plan. Emotional control involves staying grounded, maintaining humility, and adhering to the established trading rules.

3. **Controlling Greed and Fear:**

   - **Greed and Fear Dynamics:** Bollinger Bands help identify overbought and oversold conditions. Emotional control requires resisting the urge to get greedy during strong trends or panicking during sharp pullbacks. Stick to the plan and avoid emotional extremes.

4. **Mindfulness in Decision-Making:**

   - **Staying Present:** Emotional control is heightened through mindfulness. Being present in the moment, rather than dwelling on past losses or anticipating future gains, helps traders make rational decisions based on the current market conditions.

5. **Avoiding Revenge Trading:**

- **Overcoming Frustration:** Losses can lead to frustration, and revenge trading is a common emotional response. Successful traders exhibit emotional control by refraining from revenge trading, realizing that the market doesn't owe them anything.

6. **Utilizing Stress-Reduction Techniques:**

- **Mind-Body Connection:** Physical and mental well-being are interconnected. Traders can practice stress-reduction techniques such as meditation, exercise, and proper sleep to enhance emotional control and decision-making.

7. **Seeking External Support:**

- **Mental Health Awareness:** Recognizing the psychological challenges of trading, some traders benefit from seeking external support, whether through trading communities, mentors, or professional counselors. Sharing experiences and challenges can contribute to emotional resilience.

CHAPTER 18

COMMON MISTAKES TO AVOID

While Bollinger Bands can be powerful tools in trading, misinterpretation and common mistakes can lead to significant pitfalls. This chapter explores some of the most prevalent errors traders make when using Bollinger Bands and offers insights on avoiding these pitfalls.

Pitfalls in Bollinger Bands Interpretation

1. **Overlooking Market Context:**

   - **Mistake:** Failing to consider broader market conditions.

   - **Consequence:** Bollinger Bands signals should be analyzed in the context of overall market trends. Ignoring the broader environment may lead to misinterpretation and poor decision-making.

2. **Neglecting Multiple Timeframes:**

- **Mistake:** Relying solely on one timeframe for analysis.

- **Consequence:** Bollinger Bands signals can vary across different timeframes. Neglecting to consider multiple timeframes may result in missing crucial information about trend direction and potential reversals.

3. **Ignoring Confirmation Indicators:**

- **Mistake:** Failing to confirm signals with other technical indicators.

- **Consequence:** Relying solely on Bollinger Bands without confirmation from oscillators or other indicators can lead to false signals. Combining multiple tools enhances the accuracy of trading decisions.

4. **Misjudging Volatility:**

- **Mistake:** Misinterpreting volatility signals from Bollinger Bands.

- **Consequence:** Failing to adjust to changing volatility conditions may result in entering trades during periods of high risk. Traders should adapt Bollinger Bands parameters to suit varying market volatility.

5. **Chasing the Squeeze without Confirmation:**

   - **Mistake:** Entering trades solely based on a Bollinger Bands squeeze.

   - **Consequence:** A squeeze alone does not guarantee a directional move. Traders should confirm squeeze patterns with volume and additional technical indicators before entering trades.

Overtrading and Misjudging Signals

1. **Impulsive Trading Based on Bands Touch:**

   - **Mistake:** Entering trades immediately upon a touch of the upper or lower band.

   - **Consequence:** Overtrading and entering positions without confirming signals may lead to losses. Traders should exercise patience and wait for additional confirmation.

2. **Falling Victim to Short-Term Noise:**

   - **Mistake:** Reacting to short-term price fluctuations without considering the overall trend.

- **Consequence:** Misjudging short-term noise as a reversal may result in premature exits or entries. Traders should prioritize the overall trend when interpreting Bollinger Bands signals.

3. **Misinterpreting Overbought and Oversold Conditions:**

   - **Mistake:** Assuming that overbought or oversold conditions imply an immediate reversal.

   - **Consequence:** Markets can remain overbought or oversold for extended periods. Traders should use these conditions as signals for potential reversals but confirm with other indicators.

4. **Failing to Adapt to Changing Market Conditions:**

   - **Mistake:** Using a static approach without adjusting strategies to evolving markets.

   - **Consequence:** Market conditions change, and a failure to adapt may result in poor performance. Traders should regularly review and adjust their strategies based on current market dynamics.

5. **Overconfidence After Successful Trades:**

   - **Mistake:** Becoming overconfident after a series of successful trades.

- **Consequence:** Overconfidence may lead to increased risk-taking and deviating from a well-defined trading plan. Traders should maintain humility and stick to proven strategies.

CHAPTER 19

ADAPTING TO CHANGING MARKET CONDITIONS

Effectively utilizing Bollinger Bands involves recognizing and adapting to changing market conditions. This chapter explores the application of Bollinger Bands in both bull and bear markets, emphasizing the importance of adjusting strategies to suit the unique characteristics of each market phase.

Bollinger Bands in Bull and Bear Markets

1. **Bull Markets:**

   - **Characteristics:** Bull markets are characterized by rising prices, positive investor sentiment, and an overall optimistic outlook.

- **Bollinger Bands in Bull Markets:** During a bull market, prices often ride the upper band, indicating sustained upward momentum. Traders can use pullbacks to the middle band as potential entry points, aligning with the overall bullish trend.

2. **Bear Markets:**

- **Characteristics:** Bear markets are characterized by falling prices, negative sentiment, and a prevailing pessimistic outlook.

- **Bollinger Bands in Bear Markets:** In a bear market, prices may frequently touch or breach the lower band, signaling strong downward momentum. Traders can consider short entries when prices touch the upper band, anticipating potential reversals.

Adjusting Strategies for Different Market Phases

1. **Volatility Considerations:**

- **Bull Market Volatility:** In a bull market, volatility may be more subdued, and breakouts may occur with less frequency. Traders should adjust Bollinger Bands parameters to capture the relatively lower volatility while still identifying trends and potential reversals.

- **Bear Market Volatility:** In a bear market, volatility tends to increase. Traders should widen Bollinger Bands parameters to accommodate larger price swings, ensuring that strategies adapt to the heightened market uncertainty.

2. **Trend Identification:**

- **Bull Market Trends:** During a bull market, traders focus on identifying and riding the prevailing uptrend. Bollinger Bands assist in confirming the trend direction and provide entry points during pullbacks to the middle band.

- **Bear Market Trends:** In a bear market, traders shift their focus to identifying downtrends. Bollinger Bands help confirm bearish trends, with short entries near the upper band and potential exits or profit-taking during touches or breaches of the lower band.

3. **Adapting to Sideways Markets:**

- **Bull Market Sideways Phases:** Even in bull markets, there are periods of consolidation. Traders can adjust strategies by using Bollinger Bands to identify range-bound conditions, employing mean reversion strategies during these phases.

- **Bear Market Sideways Phases:** Similar to bull markets, bear markets experience periods of consolidation. Traders can adapt strategies by recognizing sideways movements and employing range-bound trading approaches.

4. **Market Regime Switching:**

- **Transitioning from Bull to Bear (and Vice Versa):** Recognizing the transition from a bull to a bear market (or vice versa) is crucial. Traders can use Bollinger Bands to identify shifts in market dynamics, adjusting strategies accordingly. For instance, tightening bands during a bull market may signal a potential shift in sentiment.

5. **Combining Bollinger Bands with Trend Indicators:**

- **Bull Market:** In a bull market, combining Bollinger Bands with trend indicators like moving averages enhances trend confirmation. Crosses of short-term moving averages above longer-term moving averages can validate upward trends.

- **Bear Market:** In a bear market, combining Bollinger Bands with trend indicators helps confirm downtrends. Moving average crossovers with the short-term moving average below the long-term moving average can reinforce bearish signals.

6. **Dynamic Position Sizing:**

- **Bull Market:** In a bull market, traders may consider slightly larger position sizes, given the overall positive sentiment. However, strict risk management principles should still be applied.

- **Bear Market:** In a bear market, traders might opt for smaller position sizes to account for increased volatility and potential for larger price swings. Stringent risk management becomes even more crucial in bearish environments.

CHAPTER 20

TRADING PLAN DEVELOPMENT

A comprehensive trading plan is the foundation of successful trading, providing structure, discipline, and a roadmap for achieving financial goals. This chapter delves into the essential elements of creating a trading plan and highlights the integration of Bollinger Bands as a key component in the decision-making process.

Creating a Comprehensive Trading Plan

1. **Define Your Trading Goals:**

    - **Financial Objectives:** Clearly articulate your financial goals, whether they involve capital growth, income generation, or capital preservation. Establish both short-term and long-term objectives to guide your trading endeavors.

2. **Risk Tolerance and Capital Allocation:**

- **Risk Tolerance Assessment:** Evaluate your risk tolerance, considering how much capital you are willing to risk on each trade. Define the maximum percentage of your trading capital you are comfortable losing on a single trade.

- **Capital Allocation:** Determine the portion of your trading capital allocated to different asset classes or strategies. Balance diversification with a focused approach based on your risk appetite.

3. **Time Commitment:**

- **Trading Frequency:** Clarify your preferred trading style, whether it's day trading, swing trading, or long-term investing. Align the time commitment with your lifestyle, ensuring it's realistic and sustainable.

- **Market Monitoring:** Specify the time you can dedicate to market analysis, research, and monitoring. This includes both pre-market preparation and post-market review.

4. **Develop Clear Entry and Exit Rules:**

- **Entry Criteria:** Define the specific criteria that must be met for entering a trade. This may include Bollinger Bands signals, confirmation from other indicators, and alignment with the overall market trend.

- **Exit Criteria:** Establish clear rules for exiting trades, encompassing profit-taking targets, stop-loss levels, and conditions signaling a potential reversal. Ensure that your exit strategy aligns with your risk-reward ratios.

5. **Risk Management Strategies:**

- **Stop-Loss Placement:** Determine where you will place stop-loss orders based on Bollinger Bands signals and other technical analysis. Adapt stop-loss levels to market conditions and volatility.

- **Position Sizing:** Develop a position sizing strategy that aligns with your risk tolerance and the volatility of the asset. Avoid over-leveraging by adhering to a consistent position sizing methodology.

6. **Market Analysis and Research:**

- **Technical and Fundamental Analysis:** Specify the tools and methodologies you will use for market analysis. Incorporate both technical analysis, such as Bollinger Bands, and fundamental analysis to make well-informed trading decisions.

- **Market News and Events:** Include a plan for staying informed about market news and economic events that may impact your trades. Set up reliable sources for timely information.

7. **Contingency Plans:**

- **Adaptability:** Acknowledge that market conditions can change. Develop contingency plans for unexpected events, market reversals, or changes in volatility. Define when and how you will adapt your strategy.

- **Review and Adapt Regularly:** Commit to regular reviews of your trading plan. Adapt the plan as needed based on your evolving experience, changes in market conditions, and performance evaluations.

Incorporating Bollinger Bands into Your Plan

1. **Bollinger Bands Parameters:**

- **Setting Parameters:** Specify the Bollinger Bands parameters you will use, including the period and standard deviation. Consider adjusting these parameters based on the asset class and prevailing market conditions.

2. **Bollinger Bands Signals:**

- **Interpretation Rules:** Clearly outline how you will interpret Bollinger Bands signals. Define conditions for potential trend reversals, breakouts, or range-bound movements based on the positioning of prices relative to the bands.

3. **Confirmation with Other Indicators:**

   - **Integrating Indicators:** Describe how you will use Bollinger Bands in conjunction with other technical indicators, such as moving averages or oscillators, to enhance signal confirmation. This multi-indicator approach strengthens decision-making.

4. **Squeeze Patterns and Breakouts:**

   - **Squeeze Recognition:** Specify criteria for recognizing Bollinger Bands squeeze patterns. Outline the actions you will take during squeeze conditions, considering potential breakout or breakdown scenarios.

   - **Breakout Strategies:** Detail your approach to trading breakouts signaled by Bollinger Bands. Define confirmation criteria and the risk management measures you will employ during breakout trades.

5. **Review and Optimization:**

- **Regular Assessment:** Establish a schedule for reviewing the effectiveness of Bollinger Bands in your trading plan. Regularly assess whether adjustments to parameters or strategies are necessary based on the evolving market environment.

- **Optimization:** Outline a systematic process for optimizing your use of Bollinger Bands. This may involve backtesting different parameter settings, evaluating the impact of varying timeframes, and adjusting strategies for different market conditions.

6. **Learning and Development:**

- **Continuous Learning:** Emphasize the importance of continuous learning in your trading plan. Commit to staying informed about new developments in technical analysis, refining your understanding of Bollinger Bands, and adapting to advancements in market analysis techniques.

CHAPTER 21

RISK MANAGEMENT STRATEGIES

Risk management is the cornerstone of successful trading, helping traders protect their capital and navigate the uncertainties of financial markets. This chapter explores essential risk management strategies, focusing on setting stop losses, establishing take profits, and employing effective position sizing techniques.

Setting Stop Losses and Take Profits

1. **Importance of Stop Losses:**

    -   **Capital Protection:** The primary purpose of a stop loss is to protect your trading capital. It defines the maximum amount of acceptable loss on a trade, preventing catastrophic losses and preserving capital for future opportunities.

2. **Determining Stop Loss Levels:**

   - **Technical Analysis:** Use technical analysis, including tools like Bollinger Bands, to identify key support and resistance levels. Place stop losses below support in long trades and above resistance in short trades.

   - **Volatility Considerations:** Adjust stop loss levels based on market volatility. In more volatile conditions, widen the stop loss to account for larger price fluctuations, and vice versa for less volatile markets.

3. **Trailing Stop Losses:**

   - **Dynamic Adjustments:** Trailing stop losses follow the price as it moves in a favorable direction. This dynamic approach allows traders to lock in profits while giving the trade room to breathe. Trailing stops can be based on fixed percentages, ATR (Average True Range), or specific technical levels.

4. **Take Profit Strategies:**

   - **Objective Setting:** Establish clear profit-taking objectives based on technical analysis and market conditions. Consider setting multiple take profit levels to secure profits incrementally as the trade progresses.

- **Market Context:** Adapt take profit strategies to the prevailing market context. In trending markets, consider letting profits run by using trailing take profits. In range-bound markets, take profits at key resistance or support levels.

5. **Risk-Reward Ratios:**

   - **Balancing Risk and Reward:** Maintain a favorable risk-reward ratio in your trades. For example, if your stop loss represents a 2% loss, ensure that your take profit objective offers at least a 4% gain. This balance helps offset losses with profitable trades over the long term.

   - **Consistency in Ratios:** Establish consistent risk-reward ratios across your trades to maintain a disciplined approach. Avoid taking trades where the potential loss exceeds the potential gain.

Position Sizing Techniques

1. **Fixed Dollar Amount:**

   - **Consistent Risk:** Set a fixed dollar amount or percentage of your trading capital as the maximum risk per trade. This approach ensures that each trade carries a consistent level of risk, regardless of the trade's size or volatility.

- **Adaptation to Capital Changes:** Adjust the fixed dollar amount as your trading capital grows or declines. This allows for flexibility while maintaining a consistent risk level.

2. **Percentage of Capital:**

- **Risk as a Percentage:** Determine a percentage of your total capital that you are willing to risk on a single trade. This method adjusts position sizes based on the size of your trading account.

- **Dynamic Position Sizing:** As your capital fluctuates, your position size adapts accordingly. This technique accommodates changes in the size of your trading account while maintaining a proportional risk level.

3. **Volatility-Based Position Sizing:**

- **ATR as a Measure:** Use the Average True Range (ATR) as a measure of market volatility. Adjust position sizes based on the ATR to account for varying levels of volatility.

- **Adaptability:** In more volatile markets, position sizes are reduced to mitigate the impact of larger price swings. In less volatile conditions, position sizes can be increased to capture potential smaller price movements.

4. **Risk Parity:**

- **Balancing Risks:** Allocate capital to trades in a way that balances the overall risk in your portfolio. Each trade contributes a proportional amount to the total risk, preventing overexposure to a single position.

- **Diversification:** Consider the risk exposure of your entire portfolio when determining the size of individual positions. Diversification across different assets or strategies contributes to risk parity.

5. **Optimal f:**

- **Kelly Criterion:** The Kelly Criterion calculates the optimal position size to maximize returns while minimizing the risk of ruin. It considers the probability of winning and losing trades, allowing for an aggressive yet disciplined approach to position sizing.

- **Cautionary Use:** Exercise caution with the Kelly Criterion, as aggressive positions can lead to significant drawdowns. Many traders prefer a more conservative approach, such as a fraction of the Kelly Criterion.

CHAPTER 22

BACKTESTING BOLLINGER BANDS STRATEGIES

Backtesting is a crucial step in evaluating the historical performance of trading strategies, including those involving Bollinger Bands. This chapter explores the significance of backtesting, providing insights into the process and tools/platforms available for conducting thorough evaluations.

Importance of Backtesting

1. **Performance Validation:**

   - **Historical Results:** Backtesting allows traders to assess how a Bollinger Bands strategy would have performed in the past. This historical perspective provides insights into the strategy's efficacy under various market conditions.

2. **Strategy Refinement:**

   - **Identifying Strengths and Weaknesses:** Backtesting helps identify the strengths and weaknesses of a Bollinger Bands strategy. By analyzing historical trades, traders can refine and optimize their strategies for improved performance.

3. **Risk Management Assessment:**

   - **Quantifying Risk:** Backtesting enables the quantification of risk and the assessment of risk management components within a strategy. This includes evaluating stop loss placement, position sizing, and overall risk-reward ratios.

4. **Psychological Preparation:**

   - **Emotional Resilience:** Experiencing the psychological aspects of trading without real capital at risk can build emotional resilience. Traders gain confidence in their strategies and learn to handle drawdowns and losing streaks with a disciplined mindset.

5. **Strategy Adaptation:**

   - **Market Conditions:** Backtesting helps traders understand how a Bollinger Bands strategy adapts to different market conditions. Strategies that prove effective in diverse scenarios are more likely to be robust and reliable in live trading.

Tools and Platforms for Backtesting

1. **Trading Platforms:**

   - **Built-In Backtesting Tools:** Many trading platforms come equipped with built-in backtesting tools. These platforms allow traders to implement and evaluate Bollinger Bands strategies using historical data, providing a seamless integration with live trading.

2. **Algorithmic Trading Platforms:**

   - **QuantConnect, Quantopian, and MetaTrader:** Algorithmic trading platforms such as QuantConnect, Quantopian, and MetaTrader offer advanced backtesting capabilities. Traders can code and test Bollinger Bands strategies in these environments, assessing performance across various timeframes and asset classes.

3. **Python Libraries:**

   - **Pandas, NumPy, and Backtrader:** Traders with coding proficiency can use Python libraries like Pandas and NumPy for data manipulation and Backtrader for backtesting. This approach offers flexibility and customization in testing Bollinger Bands strategies.

4. **Third-Party Backtesting Software:**

   - **TradeStation, AmiBroker, and NinjaTrader:** Third-party software like TradeStation, AmiBroker, and NinjaTrader provides comprehensive backtesting features. These platforms offer user-friendly interfaces and robust analytical tools for evaluating Bollinger Bands strategies.

5. **Excel Spreadsheets:**

   - **Custom Analysis:** For those who prefer a more manual approach, Excel spreadsheets can be used for backtesting Bollinger Bands strategies. Traders can input historical data, implement trading rules, and analyze performance metrics.

6. **Machine Learning Platforms:**

   - **TensorFlow, scikit-learn, and Keras:** Traders interested in machine learning can use platforms like TensorFlow, scikit-learn, and Keras for backtesting Bollinger Bands strategies. Machine learning models can be trained on historical data to optimize strategy parameters.

7. **Cloud-Based Solutions:**

- **CloudQuant, QuantConnect:** Cloud-based platforms like CloudQuant and QuantConnect offer the advantage of scalability and accessibility. Traders can backtest Bollinger Bands strategies in the cloud, leveraging computational power for more extensive analyses.

Best Practices in Backtesting Bollinger Bands Strategies:

1. **Use Adequate Historical Data:**

   - **Sufficient Timeframe:** Ensure that the backtesting period covers a sufficiently long timeframe to capture various market conditions. This helps assess the strategy's adaptability over time.

2. **Consider Transaction Costs:**

   - **Realistic Assumptions:** Incorporate realistic transaction costs and slippage into the backtesting process. This ensures that the results are more representative of actual trading conditions.

3. **Out-of-Sample Testing:**

   - **Separate Data for Validation:** Reserve a portion of the historical data for out-of-sample testing. This provides an independent dataset to validate the strategy's performance and reduces the risk of overfitting.

4. **Regularly Update Data:**

   - **Stay Current:** Regularly update historical data to include the most recent market conditions. This allows traders to adapt Bollinger Bands strategies to changing environments.

5. **Optimization vs. Overfitting:**

   - **Balancing Act:** Avoid over-optimization by striking a balance between refining strategy parameters and preventing overfitting. A strategy that is overly tuned to historical data may not perform well in live markets.

6. **Review and Refine:**

   - **Iterative Process:** Backtesting is an iterative process. Continuously review and refine Bollinger Bands strategies based on backtesting results and adapt them to evolving market conditions.

CHAPTER 23

BOLLINGER BANDS AND CRYPTOCURRENCY TRADING

Cryptocurrency markets present unique characteristics and challenges that require specific considerations when incorporating Bollinger Bands. This chapter explores the distinctive aspects of cryptocurrency trading and provides strategies tailored to the crypto environment.

Unique Considerations in Cryptocurrency Markets

1. **24/7 Market Operation:**

   - Cryptocurrency markets operate 24/7, presenting continuous price movements. Bollinger Bands can help identify trends and potential reversals in this dynamic environment. Traders should adapt their strategies to account for non-stop market activity.

2. **High Volatility:**

   - Cryptocurrencies are known for their high volatility. Bollinger Bands, with their ability to measure volatility, become crucial in identifying potential price breakouts or breakdowns. Adjust Bollinger Bands parameters to accommodate the pronounced price swings in crypto markets.

3. **Liquidity Variability:**

   - Liquidity in cryptocurrency markets can vary significantly. Bollinger Bands can aid in assessing liquidity levels and potential slippage. Traders should exercise caution and adjust position sizes accordingly, especially in less liquid altcoins.

4. **News Sensitivity:**

   - Cryptocurrency prices are highly sensitive to news and events. Bollinger Bands can be used to gauge the market's reaction to news releases. Consider incorporating additional fundamental analysis alongside Bollinger Bands to navigate the impact of external factors on crypto prices.

5. **Lack of Regulation:**

- The cryptocurrency market is less regulated than traditional financial markets. This lack of oversight can lead to sudden and unpredictable price movements. Bollinger Bands can assist in identifying abnormal price behavior, aiding traders in risk management.

Cryptocurrency-Specific Strategies

1. **Bollinger Bands Squeeze in Cryptocurrencies:**

- **Recognition:** Identify Bollinger Bands squeezes, which indicate periods of low volatility and potential upcoming price movements. Cryptocurrency markets often experience explosive moves following a squeeze.

- **Confirmation:** Confirm squeeze patterns with volume analysis and additional indicators. A surge in volume during a breakout from a squeeze enhances the reliability of the signal.

2. **Breakout and Breakdown Trading:**

- **Volatility Breakouts:** Cryptocurrencies frequently experience significant price breakouts. Bollinger Bands help traders identify potential breakout points, especially when prices touch or surpass the outer bands.

- **Confirmation Indicators:** Combine Bollinger Bands with confirmation indicators such as the Relative Strength Index (RSI) or Moving Average Convergence Divergence (MACD) for added confirmation before entering breakout trades.

3. **Trend Identification in Cryptocurrencies:**

- **Adaptation to Crypto Trends:** Cryptocurrencies exhibit strong trends. Bollinger Bands help identify and confirm these trends. Look for sustained moves towards the upper or lower bands as potential indications of the prevailing trend.

- **Support and Resistance:** Bollinger Bands act as dynamic support and resistance levels. Use these levels in conjunction with other technical analysis tools to refine entry and exit points in trending markets.

4. **Altcoin Strategies with Bollinger Bands:**

- **Volatility-Based Selection:** Given the varied liquidity and volatility of altcoins, use Bollinger Bands to screen and select candidates for trading. Prioritize altcoins with clear Bollinger Bands signals and established trends.

- **Diversification:** Cryptocurrency portfolios often include a mix of major coins and altcoins. Diversify strategies based on Bollinger Bands across different cryptocurrencies to spread risk and capitalize on varied market movements.

5. **Risk Management in Cryptocurrency Trading:**

- **Dynamic Stop Losses:** Cryptocurrencies can experience rapid price swings. Implement dynamic stop losses based on Bollinger Bands and adjust them in response to changing volatility conditions.

- **Position Sizing:** Due to the potential for extreme volatility, carefully consider position sizes. Bollinger Bands, with their ability to measure volatility, can guide traders in adapting position sizes to the risk inherent in cryptocurrency markets.

6. **News-Driven Trading with Bollinger Bands:**

- **News Reaction Signals:** Cryptocurrencies often react sharply to news events. Bollinger Bands can help identify potential entry and exit points during these volatile periods. Wait for confirmation signals before acting on news-driven price movements.

- **Quick Reversal Analysis:** Bollinger Bands assist in quickly identifying potential reversals following sharp price movements caused by news events. Traders can use the bands to gauge when a rapid move might be overextended.

CHAPTER 24

ADVANCED CHARTING TECHNIQUES

Beyond traditional candlestick charts, advanced charting techniques offer unique perspectives on price action. This chapter explores three distinctive charting methods—Renko charts, Heikin-Ashi charts, and Point and Figure charts—providing insights into their construction, interpretation, and application in trading.

Renko Charts

1. **Definition and Construction:**

   - **Renko Basics:** Renko charts represent price movements in bricks or "blocks" rather than time intervals. A new brick is formed only when the price moves a predefined amount (the box size) in either direction.

- **Construction:** Bricks are either drawn as hollow or filled, depending on the direction of price movement. The chart smoothens market noise and emphasizes trends.

2. **Interpretation:**

   - **Trend Identification:** Renko charts are excellent for trend identification. An upward trend is indicated by a series of ascending filled bricks, while a descending trend is shown by descending hollow bricks.

   - **Reversal Signals:** Reversal signals are generated when the bricks change direction, providing traders with insights into potential trend shifts.

3. **Applications in Trading:**

   - **Support and Resistance:** Renko charts help identify clear support and resistance levels, often providing a cleaner picture compared to traditional charts.

   - **Filtering Noise:** By focusing on significant price movements, Renko charts filter out noise and highlight sustained trends.

Heikin-Ashi Charts

1. **Definition and Construction:**

- **Candlestick Variation:** Heikin-Ashi, translating to "average bar" in Japanese, is a modified candlestick charting technique.

- **Construction:** Each Heikin-Ashi candle is calculated based on the average prices of the current period, providing a smoother representation of price action.

2. **Interpretation:**

- **Trend Identification:** Heikin-Ashi charts are adept at trend identification. Bullish trends are characterized by predominantly green candles, while bearish trends feature mostly red candles.

- **Candlestick Patterns:** Traditional candlestick patterns may appear differently on Heikin-Ashi charts, influencing the interpretation of market sentiment.

3. **Applications in Trading:**

- **Trend Confirmation:** Heikin-Ashi helps confirm trends and reduces the impact of market noise, making it easier for traders to identify the prevailing market sentiment.

- **Signal Confirmation:** Heikin-Ashi can be used in conjunction with traditional candlestick patterns and technical indicators to confirm signals and enhance trading decisions.

Point and Figure Charts

1. **Definition and Construction:**

    - **Unique Charting System:** Point and Figure charts differ significantly from traditional charts, representing price movements with Xs and Os.

    - **Construction:** Xs denote rising prices, while Os represent falling prices. The chart focuses solely on price changes, disregarding time.

2. **Interpretation:**

    - **Trend Identification:** Point and Figure charts excel at identifying trends. Columns of Xs or Os form as prices trend in one direction, providing a clear visual representation.

    - **Reversal Patterns:** Reversal patterns, such as double tops or bottoms, are easily identified on Point and Figure charts.

3. **Applications in Trading:**

    - **Support and Resistance:** Point and Figure charts help identify support and resistance levels. Breakouts from these levels are considered significant signals.

    - **Volatility Measurement:** Box sizes and reversal amounts in Point and Figure charts can be adjusted to accommodate different levels of volatility.

Choosing the Right Charting Technique:

1. **Timeframe and Trading Style:**

    - **Day Trading:** Traders focusing on intraday moves may find Renko charts helpful for filtering noise.

    - **Swing Trading:** Heikin-Ashi charts can assist swing traders in identifying and confirming trends.

    - **Long-Term Investing:** Point and Figure charts may be beneficial for long-term investors seeking to identify major trends and reversal patterns.

2. **Market Conditions:**

    - **Trending Markets:** Renko charts and Point and Figure charts are well-suited for trending markets.

    - **Volatility:** Heikin-Ashi charts may be useful in volatile markets to smooth out price fluctuations.

3. **Combining Techniques:**

- **Comprehensive Analysis:** Traders may combine these advanced charting techniques with traditional charts and technical indicators for a more comprehensive analysis.

- **Confirmation:** Using multiple chart types can provide confirmation signals, enhancing the robustness of trading decisions.

CHAPTER 25

BOLLINGER BANDS AND ECONOMIC INDICATORS

Understanding the relationship between Bollinger Bands and economic indicators is crucial for traders seeking to navigate the complexities of financial markets influenced by economic data. This chapter explores the impact of economic indicators on Bollinger Bands and provides insights into trading strategies around significant economic events.

Impact of Economic Data on Bollinger Bands

1. **Volatility Surges:**

   - **Economic Releases:** Major economic indicators, such as GDP reports, employment numbers, and inflation data, can lead to sudden and substantial market movements.

- **Bollinger Bands Response:** Bollinger Bands react to increased volatility by expanding. Traders can observe widening bands as a visual representation of heightened market uncertainty following the release of economic data.

2. **Trend Development:**

   - **Market Sentiment Shifts:** Economic indicators often influence market sentiment, causing shifts in the prevailing trend.

   - **Bollinger Bands Confirmation:** Bollinger Bands can assist in confirming trend changes following the release of economic data. A sustained move beyond the bands may signal the development of a new trend.

3. **Reversal Opportunities:**

   - **Overreaction to Data:** Markets may overreact to economic data initially, creating potential reversal opportunities.

   - **Bollinger Bands as Reversal Indicators:** Bollinger Bands help traders identify potential reversal points as prices move beyond the bands. Reversion to the mean strategies can be applied in these situations.

Trading Around Economic Events

1. **Pre-Event Preparations:**

   - **Calendar Monitoring:** Keep a close eye on economic calendars to be aware of upcoming releases.

   - **Adjusting Positions:** Consider adjusting position sizes or placing protective stops ahead of major economic announcements to manage risk.

2. **Interpreting Bollinger Bands During Events:**

   - **Immediate Post-Release Analysis:** Watch Bollinger Bands closely immediately after the release of economic data for signs of volatility and potential trend development.

   - **Confirmation with Other Indicators:** Use additional technical indicators alongside Bollinger Bands to confirm signals and enhance the accuracy of market analysis.

3. **Volatility Trading Strategies:**

   - **Straddle or Strangle Options Strategies:** Options traders may employ straddle or strangle strategies to capitalize on the expected volatility around economic events.

   - **Volatility Index (VIX) Confirmation:** Monitor the VIX, which reflects market volatility expectations. A rising VIX may align with widening Bollinger Bands, indicating increased volatility.

4. **Reversal Strategies:**

- **Wait for Confirmation:** Following an initial market reaction to economic data, wait for confirmation signals using Bollinger Bands before considering reversal trades.

- **Contrarian Approaches:** Bollinger Bands can be valuable for contrarian traders looking to capitalize on overreactions to economic events.

5. **Trend Continuation Opportunities:**

- **Trend Confirmation:** Use Bollinger Bands to confirm the continuation of an existing trend after economic data releases.

- **Avoid Chasing Prices:** Exercise caution and avoid chasing prices in the immediate aftermath of economic events. Wait for confirmation signals to reduce the risk of entering false trends.

6. **Risk Management:**

- **Protective Stops:** Implement protective stops to manage risk, especially during periods of heightened volatility.

- **Position Sizing:** Adjust position sizes based on the expected impact of economic events. Smaller positions may be prudent when uncertainty is high.

7. **Long-Term Economic Trends:**

   - **Bollinger Bands on Longer Timeframes:** Apply Bollinger Bands on longer timeframes to assess the impact of economic data on long-term trends.

   - **Macro Analysis:** Incorporate Bollinger Bands into a broader macroeconomic analysis to identify potential shifts in economic trends.

CHAPTER 26

REGULATORY CONSIDERATIONS

In the world of trading and investing, adherence to regulations is paramount. This chapter explores the crucial aspects of compliance, regulations, and the importance of staying informed about market changes to ensure a secure and ethical trading environment.

Compliance and Regulations in Trading

1. **Regulatory Authorities:**

   - **SEC (U.S. Securities and Exchange Commission):** In the United States, the SEC oversees securities and financial markets, enforcing regulations to protect investors.

- **FCA (Financial Conduct Authority):** The FCA in the UK regulates financial markets and firms, promoting transparency and fairness.

- **ESMA (European Securities and Markets Authority):** ESMA works to enhance investor protection and promote stable financial markets across the European Union.

2. **Key Regulatory Aspects:**

- **Insider Trading:** Trading on non-public information is illegal. Traders must avoid using confidential information for personal gain.

- **Market Manipulation:** Deliberate actions to mislead the market or create artificial pricing are strictly prohibited.

- **AML (Anti-Money Laundering) Compliance:** Traders must comply with AML regulations to prevent the use of financial systems for illicit activities.

3. **Broker Regulation:**

- **Choosing a Regulated Broker:** Select brokers regulated by reputable authorities to ensure a secure trading environment.

- **Account Protection:** Regulated brokers often offer account protection measures, such as segregating client funds from operational funds.

4. **Record-Keeping Requirements:**

- **Transaction Records:** Maintain detailed records of all trades, including transaction dates, prices, and volumes.

- **Account Statements:** Regularly review and retain account statements for compliance and auditing purposes.

Staying Informed about Market Changes

1. **Regulatory Updates:**

- **Subscription to Regulatory Notices:** Subscribe to updates and notices from relevant regulatory authorities to stay informed about changes in regulations.

- **Legal Counsel Consultation:** Regularly consult with legal professionals to ensure compliance with evolving regulatory requirements.

2. **Market Structure Changes:**

- **Algorithmic Trading Rules:** Stay informed about changes in regulations related to algorithmic trading, as this area is subject to continuous development.

- **High-Frequency Trading (HFT) Guidelines:** Regulations around HFT may evolve; traders engaging in high-frequency strategies should be aware of any changes affecting their activities.

3. **Crypto and Digital Asset Regulations:**

- **Evolution of Crypto Regulations:** As the regulatory landscape for cryptocurrencies evolves, stay informed about developments that may impact trading in digital assets.

- **Compliance with KYC (Know Your Customer) and AML in Crypto:** Regulations around KYC and AML in the crypto space may change; adhere to the latest requirements to ensure compliance.

4. **Global Regulatory Alignment:**

- **Cross-Border Trading Considerations:** For traders engaging in cross-border activities, be aware of regulatory nuances in different jurisdictions.

- **Regulatory Harmonization:** Stay informed about efforts toward global regulatory harmonization, which can impact the ease of international trading.

5. **Educational Resources:**

- **Regulatory Webinars and Seminars:** Attend webinars and seminars hosted by regulatory bodies to gain insights into upcoming changes and best practices.

- **Industry Conferences:** Participate in industry conferences where regulatory updates are often discussed, providing an opportunity for networking and knowledge-sharing.

6. **Technology and Compliance:**

- **Utilizing Compliance Software:** Leverage technology solutions designed to facilitate compliance and regulatory reporting.

- **Cybersecurity Compliance:** Stay vigilant about evolving cybersecurity regulations to protect against cyber threats and ensure the security of trading platforms.

CHAPTER 27

FUTURE DEVELOPMENTS IN BOLLINGER BANDS

The realm of trading and technical analysis is dynamic, and Bollinger Bands continue to be a versatile tool for traders. This chapter explores potential future developments in Bollinger Bands, including emerging trends, technologies, and the evolution of trading strategies.

Emerging Trends and Technologies

1. **Artificial Intelligence (AI) Integration:**

   - *Predictive Analytics:* AI algorithms could be employed to enhance Bollinger Bands by providing predictive analytics, allowing traders to anticipate potential price movements with greater accuracy.

- *Pattern Recognition:* AI-powered systems may improve pattern recognition within Bollinger Bands, enabling the identification of complex market patterns that are challenging for traditional methods.

2. **Machine Learning Applications:**

- *Dynamic Parameter Optimization:* Machine learning algorithms could optimize Bollinger Bands parameters dynamically based on current market conditions, adapting to changing volatility and trend characteristics.

- *Automated Pattern Recognition:* Machine learning models may automate the recognition of Bollinger Bands patterns, reducing the cognitive load on traders and improving the efficiency of strategy implementation.

3. **Blockchain and Cryptocurrency Integration:**

- *Decentralized Trading Platforms:* As blockchain technology advances, decentralized trading platforms may incorporate Bollinger Bands as part of their technical analysis tools, providing a seamless experience for cryptocurrency traders.

- *Smart Contracts for Trading Strategies:* Smart contracts on blockchain networks could be used to execute trading strategies automatically when predefined Bollinger Bands conditions are met, enhancing the efficiency and transparency of trading.

4. **Quantum Computing Impact:**

   - *Complex Analysis:* Quantum computing's ability to process vast amounts of data simultaneously may open avenues for more complex and sophisticated analysis within the realm of Bollinger Bands, potentially leading to more accurate predictions.

   - *Algorithm Optimization:* Quantum algorithms may optimize trading algorithms associated with Bollinger Bands, allowing for faster computations and more intricate strategy development.

Evolution of Trading Strategies

1. **Algorithmic Trading Advancements:**

   - *High-Frequency Trading (HFT) Strategies:* Further advancements in algorithmic trading may lead to more sophisticated HFT strategies that leverage Bollinger Bands for rapid decision-making in volatile markets.

   - *Multi-Asset Algorithmic Strategies:* Algorithmic trading strategies incorporating Bollinger Bands may expand to cover a broader range of asset classes, providing diversification opportunities for automated trading systems.

2. **Integration with Fundamental Analysis:**

   - *Dynamic Fusion of Data:* Traders may increasingly integrate Bollinger Bands with fundamental data through advanced analytics, providing a more holistic view of market conditions and enhancing decision-making.

   - *Sentiment Analysis Integration:* Bollinger Bands could be incorporated into trading strategies that utilize sentiment analysis, combining technical and fundamental factors for a comprehensive approach.

3. **Personalized Trading Strategies:**

   - *AI-Driven Personalization:* AI algorithms may enable the creation of personalized trading strategies based on individual risk tolerance, preferences, and historical performance with Bollinger Bands as a key component.

   - *Behavioral Analysis:* Future developments might involve integrating behavioral analysis into trading strategies, adapting Bollinger Bands signals based on individual trader behavior and decision patterns.

4. **Global Macro Strategies:**

- *Macroeconomic Data Integration:* Trading strategies involving Bollinger Bands may evolve to incorporate a more significant emphasis on global macroeconomic factors, providing a broader context for decision-making.

- *Cross-Asset Class Analysis:* Traders may develop strategies that consider Bollinger Bands signals across multiple asset classes simultaneously, recognizing interconnected trends and patterns.

CHAPTER 28

RESOURCES AND TOOLS FOR BOLLINGER BANDS ANALYSIS

Successful Bollinger Bands analysis requires a solid foundation of knowledge and the right tools. This chapter explores recommended books, online courses and webinars, as well as trading platforms and software that can aid traders in mastering Bollinger Bands and enhancing their technical analysis skills.

Recommended Books

1. **"Bollinger on Bollinger Bands" by John Bollinger:**

   - *Authoritative Guide:* Written by the creator of Bollinger Bands, John Bollinger, this book provides in-depth insights into the indicator's construction, interpretation, and various strategies. It's a must-read for those seeking a comprehensive understanding of Bollinger Bands.

2. **"Technical Analysis of the Financial Markets" by John J. Murphy:**

   - *Comprehensive Reference:* While not solely focused on Bollinger Bands, Murphy's book is a comprehensive guide to technical analysis. It covers various indicators, including Bollinger Bands, offering a broader perspective on technical analysis principles.

3. **"The Encyclopedia of Chart Patterns" by Thomas N. Bulkowski:**

   - *Pattern Recognition:* Bulkowski's book delves into chart patterns, complementing Bollinger Bands analysis. It provides a valuable resource for traders looking to combine pattern recognition with Bollinger Bands strategies.

Online Courses and Webinars

1. **Investopedia Academy - Bollinger Bands Course:**

   - *Structured Learning:* Investopedia Academy offers a course specifically dedicated to Bollinger Bands. This course provides a structured approach to understanding and applying Bollinger Bands in trading.

2. **Coursera - Technical Analysis and Trading Ideas by Indian School of Business:**

   - *Comprehensive Coverage:* This course on Coursera covers technical analysis, including Bollinger Bands, and provides practical trading ideas. It's suitable for both beginners and intermediate-level traders.

3. **Webinars by TradingView:**

   - *Live Learning:* TradingView often hosts webinars on various technical analysis topics, including Bollinger Bands. Attending these live sessions allows traders to interact with experts, ask questions, and deepen their understanding of Bollinger Bands.

Trading Platforms and Software

1. **TradingView:**

   - *User-Friendly Platform:* TradingView is a popular online platform that integrates advanced charting tools, including Bollinger Bands. It allows users to customize charts, apply technical indicators, and share trading ideas within a community of traders.

2. **Thinkorswim by TD Ameritrade:**

   - *Advanced Charting:* Thinkorswim is known for its advanced charting capabilities. It offers customizable studies, including Bollinger Bands, and provides a paper trading feature for users to practice their strategies.

3. **MetaTrader 4 (MT4) and MetaTrader 5 (MT5):**

- *Algorithmic Trading Support:* MT4 and MT5 are widely used platforms that support algorithmic trading. Traders can apply Bollinger Bands and develop custom indicators or automated strategies using MetaEditor.

4. **NinjaTrader:**

- *Advanced Analysis Tools:* NinjaTrader is a trading platform that provides advanced analysis tools. It supports Bollinger Bands, and traders can develop and test strategies using the NinjaScript development environment.

5. **Python with Pandas and Matplotlib/Plotly:**

- *Custom Analysis:* For traders with programming skills, using Python with Pandas for data manipulation and Matplotlib or Plotly for visualization offers a powerful way to customize Bollinger Bands analysis and integrate it into algorithmic trading strategies.

CHAPTER 29

CONCLUSION AND FINAL THOUGHTS

As we conclude this comprehensive exploration of Bollinger Bands and their applications in trading, it's essential to sum up key concepts and provide encouragement for continuous learning and improvement in the dynamic world of financial markets.

Summing Up Key Concepts

1. **Bollinger Bands Basics:**

   - *Definition:* Bollinger Bands consist of an upper band, a lower band, and a middle band. The upper and lower bands are based on standard deviations from a moving average, reflecting price volatility.

2. **Interpretation of Bollinger Bands:**

- *Volatility and Trend Identification:* Bollinger Bands help traders identify periods of high or low volatility and recognize trends. The width of the bands can be indicative of market conditions.

- *Overbought and Oversold Conditions:* Prices approaching the upper band may indicate overbought conditions, while prices near the lower band may suggest oversold conditions.

3. **Bollinger Bands Strategies:**

- *Squeeze and Breakout Patterns:* Recognizing squeeze patterns can signal potential explosive price movements. Breakouts from the bands can be used to identify trend reversals or continuations.

- *Reversal Strategies:* Bollinger Bands can assist in identifying potential reversal points, particularly when prices deviate significantly from the bands.

4. **Advanced Strategies and Tools:**

- *Combination with Other Indicators:* Traders often combine Bollinger Bands with other indicators such as moving averages, RSI, and MACD for confirmation signals.

- *Multiple Timeframe Analysis:* Applying Bollinger Bands across different timeframes enhances trend identification and provides a broader perspective on market dynamics.

5. **Risk Management and Psychology:**

   - *Discipline and Patience:* Successful trading with Bollinger Bands requires discipline and patience. Avoid impulsive decisions and stick to well-defined strategies.

   - *Position Sizing:* Implement sound risk management practices, including setting appropriate stop-loss levels and sizing positions based on risk tolerance.

6. **Continuous Learning:**

   - *Adaptability:* The financial markets are dynamic, and strategies that once worked may need adjustments. Stay adaptable and be willing to evolve with changing market conditions.

   - *Integration of New Technologies:* Embrace advancements in technology, including AI, machine learning, and blockchain, to enhance Bollinger Bands analysis and trading strategies.

Encouragement for Continuous Learning and Improvement

1. **Stay Informed:**

- *Market Developments:* Regularly update your knowledge on market trends, economic indicators, and regulatory changes that may impact trading strategies involving Bollinger Bands.

- *Educational Resources:* Continuously explore new books, online courses, and webinars to stay informed about the latest tools and techniques in technical analysis.

2. **Practice and Experiment:**

- *Paper Trading:* Practice your strategies through paper trading or simulation platforms to refine your skills without risking real capital.

- *Experiment with Parameters:* Test different parameters for Bollinger Bands and explore how changes in settings impact their effectiveness in various market conditions.

3. **Community Engagement:**

- *Networking:* Engage with the trading community to share insights, discuss strategies, and learn from others' experiences with Bollinger Bands.

- *Online Forums and Social Media:* Participate in online forums and social media groups where traders share ideas, analysis, and tips related to Bollinger Bands.

4. **Reflect and Learn from Experience:**

    - *Trade Journaling:* Maintain a trade journal to document your trades, strategies, and the outcomes. Regularly review and reflect on your experiences to identify areas for improvement.

    - *Learn from Mistakes:* Embrace mistakes as learning opportunities. Analyze losing trades to understand what went wrong and adjust your approach accordingly.

www.ingramcontent.com/pod-product-compliance
Lightning Source LLC
Chambersburg PA
CBHW072210290526
45794CB00004B/1714